Terms and Conditions

LEGAL NOTICE

The Publisher has strived to be as accurate and complete as possible in the creation of this report, notwithstanding the fact that he does not warrant or represent at any time that the contents within are accurate due to the rapidly changing nature of the Internet.

While all attempts have been made to verify information provided in this publication, the Publisher assumes no responsibility for errors, omissions, or contrary interpretation of the subject matter herein. Any perceived slights of specific persons, peoples, or organizations are unintentional.

In practical advice books, like anything else in life, there are no guarantees of income made. Readers are cautioned to reply on their own judgment about their individual circumstances to act accordingly.

This book is not intended for use as a source of legal, business, accounting or financial advice. All readers are advised to seek services of competent professionals in legal, business, accounting and finance fields.

You are encouraged to print this book for easy reading.

Table Of Contents

Foreword

Chapter 1:
The Most Important Thing When Writing An E-book

Chapter 2:
How To Craft The Best Topic For Your Product To Catch The Attention Of Buyers

Chapter 3:
Drafting Out Your Table Of Contents

Chapter 4:
Writing It Yourself versus Outsourcing

Chapter 5:
How To Outsource

Chapter 6:
Dealing With People You Hire To Create Your Product

Chapter 7:
Developing A Long Term Working Relationship With The People You Outsource To

Wrapping Up

Foreword

There's some great news... which is you don't have to be super-creative to produce your own unique product. You may always do what so many others do, and that's to upgrade something that exists; or make it greater and better it. You may produce a product mash-up and produce something over your own. Example, you've some particular issue or subject, and you have 3 or 4 ebooks on that issue.

You may simply take ideas from all these ebooks and produce your own. You don't copy but instead learning from them and making a product of your own that lets in your own ideas, analysis and data.

The thing here is that you're handling these research products as a commencing point to get ideas, so that it becomes simple for you to work with your own product. There's an unbelievable amount of ideas simply sitting all over the place, so do keep an awareness. If you're going to build a product, then it's in your best interest to make a high quality product holding useful info.

Your first product, regardless what you do, will always take the longest and feel like the hardest. Given here are hints that will help you in that field.

The Guide To Simple And Effective Product Creation

Chapter 1:
The Most Important Thing When Writing An E-book

Synopsis

There are a lot of advantages to writing ebooks, but the experience is priceless. Authoring something so involved is truly worth the time and effort, not simply for apportioning your knowledge, but for the feedback you get from those who read it.

All the same, when most individuals begin to think about composing an entire eBook, they make the error of believing it will be complicated. The key component for success with any eBook is authoring it and presenting it the right way to your intended audience.

What You Need To Know

It's crucial to be centered if you wish to compose an eBook that will bring in cash. This is the most crucial thing about authoring a great eBook: don't let your attention wander from your goal as the more data that you are able to include in your eBook the greater it will be. For instance, if you're composing an eBook about "cat training" you have to stick to that matter and not attempt to cover everything about cats.

If an individual chooses to purchase an eBook online, they're frequently looking for very directed info that may be utilized immediately. They don't wish to go through a whole bunch of frivolity before getting to the info they require.

Additionally, bear in mind that the caliber of your eBook relies on how well you produce it. Among the chief reasons why publishers reject books again and again is because they're written poorly. So if you wish to give your target audience something they'll like, along with great info, your presentation likewise matters.

No one will give your eBook very much credit or even wish to read if it is not composed in a professional fashion. You have to really certain of what you write and how you're delivering it.

Make certain that you're specific when you ask other people to review your eBook. Would you like review of your spelling and grammar? Or about the flux and the consistency? How about the caliber and usability of your info? You have to be extremely specific when you're inviting feedback from individuals so that you know what precisely are the changes that you have to make. Remember, authoring a great

eBook takes work and time and that means that you have to take the feedback you get to heart and put it to use.

Platform

"Platform" is the publishing hoopla for a plan that you've developed to market your eBook once you've released it. Your platform consolidates a number of tools to circulate the word about your new or newest eBook. As the responsibility for marketing your book is mostly your own, you're not only the writer; you're your own publisher, also. In and of itself, you're totally in charge of getting the word out to anybody you wish to purchase and read your eBook.

As an eBook, published electronically for a likely readership that will get it, store it and read it is in an electronic data format, it stands to reason that you can reach that likely readership by electronic means. Here are a few of the things I've utilized to advertize my eBooks:

Review Books

Amazon and Barnes and Noble both enable me to provide a two-week lending of my book to a target area list of likely book reviewers associated with papers, magazines and blogs, who may help me to circulate the word about my eBook.

Smashwords goes beyond that: by their unparalleled couponing program, they let me send net coupons to this same target market, who may issue an indifferent review of my eBook for their particular readership. My blended target market reviewers get through to a potential huge readership nationwide.

Releases

In order to accomplish my plan for book reviewer and book purchaser recruitment, I formulate numerous press releases tailored to each particular demographic or geographic section.

Writer and Book Pages

Each of my selected publishers provides me with a free writer page and a separate marketing page for each of my eBooks, which enable me to provide relevant info about my eBooks and my pertinent background, likewise links to my appropriate blogs and an chance to sample and (hopefully) sell my eBook.

I utilize 2 of my blogs, to advertize any fresh developments about my eBooks. If you're an author and/or a writer, I strongly advocate that you take up blogging. It's an awesome way to express yourself on a steady basis, and it's not as hard as you may believe. As a matter of fact, WordPress.com makes it really simple with stepwise tutorials and ready-made, neat and clean templates that take all the hard stuff out of it. Likewise, WordPress blogs tend to bear very few W3C Validation errors, which aids in maximizing SEO.

Social Sites

This is an area that I'm starting to develop for my marketing technique. Right now, I'm limiting myself to Facebook and LinkedIn. On Facebook, I'm acquiring better results, and I'm building more of a fan base of loved ones and acquaintances, and of acquaintances of acquaintances. Facebook enables me to issue news about my publishing efforts, full of images and direct links to particular posts on my blog.

E-Mail Marketing

In planning for advertizing my eBooks, I acquired an extensive list of e-mail contacts, categorized into groups: loved ones, acquaintances, fellow publishers, paper editors, magazine editors, bloggers, book reviewers, and so forth. These sub-lists enabled me to tailor-make my promotional messages suitably to every group.

Publish More Than A Single Ebook

Publish more than one eBook, and publish a list of every one of your earlier eBook titles on the title page of every succeeding eBook that you publish.

Utilize a Pro Cover Designer

It's taken for granted that, particularly in the eBook publishing business, your cover picture sells your book. I'm exceedingly fortunate to have a designer who's a really talented and experienced family member who is a graphic designer. Even if you're not so lucky, I advocate you do whatever it takes to get a pro digital front cover image for your eBook. You'll need it if you wish to publish on iPad and a few of the other major eReader formats.

Chapter 2:

How To Craft The Best Topic For Your Product To Catch The Attention Of Buyers

Synopsis

Sites target to better their popularity as this means larger earnings for them. If you own a site and are working on developing a product and are wondering how to better your popularity, then you ought to learn how to use keyword search right.

Keywords are utilized to direct potential buyers to your site. The search engine rely one keywords and finds sites that have these keywords in their pages.

But with a lot of words that are utilized daily, and 1000000s of potential buyers utilizing the web, how may you be assured that the keyword you chose will help you develop a popular product? How do you know that you're targeting the correct buyers? How may you return more income through picking the correct keyword search? Worry no longer. Here are helpful hints to help you attract potential buyers and develop a product.

Getting The Product Ideas

Your finest subject is forever a subject you've passion for, knowledge with and experience with. Your personal lifetime experiences have taught you an unparalleled set of lessons. Ascertain what you know that other people may determine as valuable.

Naturally, you are able to make a small web site that centers on almost any matter you wish but you'll have a greater chance of success, particularly if this is your 1st web site or product, if you pick out a subject you have a little experience with. Additionally it makes the procedure much more fun.

Brainstorming

Begin by brainstorming a list of issues. Get a pad and pen.

What are you passionate about? Put it down. What do you like to discuss? What do you study about? What specified knowledge do you have from your line of work? Any spare-time activity? Begin writing. Put everything down…don't exclude anything, simply put it down.

List the ten greatest troubles you are able to think of in your household, work or community. What do you love doing with your free time?

Ask your acquaintances and loved ones what they think you're great at and intimate with. You may be amazed at the things they see that you've left out.

Spend a strong thirty minutes on this brainstorming time. At first the thoughts will come rapidly. But then, after you've already put down the conspicuous ones, you'll begin to have to truly think about it. This is when the true might of this exercise occurs.

You see, the subconscious is an amusing thing. It takes a steady demand from your conscious mind to acquire its attention. But when you do, your subconscious mind will take up the effort for you and start to provide answers to your question as it comes up with them.

By spending an undivided thirty minutes intensely centered on brainstorming issues for your product you transmit this demand to your subconscious. For the next week your subconscious will supply really creative topics for you in a sporadic and apparently random way. You'll be driving, taking a shower or eating supper and abruptly you'll get an awesome idea for a product.

This strategy may be utilized for almost any question or dilemma. Simply remember the energy is in the results your subconscious produces in the days after doing the exercise. And that won't occur if you don't focus intensely on brainstorming issues for an undivided half-hour. It takes this long to be sure your subconscious gets your message.

Creating Your Product

To create your product, you have to do a couple of things right in order to get top results from your work, and missing one of them may destroy your odds of being successful.

1. Find an existing market

You have to center on a group of purchasers you are able to relate to and truly comprehend. A great target market is a group of individuals who share the same basic troubles, have cash to spend, and have a history of purchasing stuff related to the issue. When you detect such a group, they're willing to purchase.

2. You has to discover what it is they already wish to purchase

You ought to sell the particular things individuals wish to purchase. Never guess when producing net business ideas. Rather, research existing products and ask individuals directly what they're seeking. As soon as you know what it is your target market is following, you'll easily be able to produce your winning product rapidly and know for certain whether it will be fruitful.

3. Produce a winning sales procedure

As soon as you have your product theme prepared, it's time to issue a basic yet effective sales letter that demonstrates what advantages your buyers will get when they purchase from you. All you have to do is tell them precisely what troubles they'll solve, promise particular end results, and ultimately make them an offer that's too good to decline.

4. You have to have targeted traffic

Now that you've your sales machine ready, it's time to begin selling. Research where your buyers may be found, and put your sales content in these places. If you are able to return at least $0.50 for every visitor, you have a success. You should then center on reaching 1000s

of individuals daily. If not, simply edit your sales presentation till it works better.

5. You has to have an effective back-end design

You have to maximize the lifespan value of every buyer. The first sale is simply to eliminate marketing costs. After that your true profits start. It's time to continually line up fresh offers that they wish to purchase from you. You are able to produce your own or make simple reseller deals with additional sellers. Simply make certain that you send a fresh offer at least once per month.

Using Keywords

Utilize Google.com

Keyword selection plays a really vital role in your net business and product research. You always have to pick out keywords that attract likelier buyers. One really valuable tool to utilize is Google.com. Google has a keyword tool named Google AdWords' Keyword tool. Begin your keyword search utilizing this link;

adwords.google.com/select/KeywordTool external.

The aim here is to pay attention to keywords that are related to your product. When picking out, target words that contain "ready-buyers" or additional words or phrases that shows commercial intensions. Include the term "ready-buyer" or any additional associated term to your selected keyword that's related to your product. For instance, in keyword tool, type "sales course best selling".

ClickBank.com net marketplace

This site specializes in digital commodities and is really popular among net marketers. Explore keywords at clickbank.com/marketplace.htm.

This site is really helpful, particularly if the products you provide relates to info, guide materials, or software. This isn't as popular as Google.com, but is a great alternative to seek the better products and services sold.

You've the option to search by product or by location. You may then narrow down search according to gravity, popularity, and the like. It's even more effective if you utilize this tool together with the gratis research tool provided by Google. Again, find terms or phrases that are akin to "ready=buyer" when searching keywords.

Shopping.com search

Once again, our target here is to seek keywords that are associated to "ready-buyers". Commercial words are the sort of keywords we're seeking. Consequently, Shopping.com is an excellent tool to utilize when searching for the correct keyword.

The finest way to detect likely buyers to find a good product online is to use the keywords that this site uses. Target keywords like clothes, accessories, books, and additional merchandise you may see on Shopping.com. If you want to offer one of these products, then this search engine is of big help to you. This is a really unique strategy that few people know.

Chapter 3:
Drafting Out Your Table Of Contents

Synopsis

A table of contents, commonly headed merely "Contents" and shortened informally as TOC, is a list of the components of a book or document prepared in the order in which the pieces appear.

The contents commonly includes the titles or descriptions of the first-level headers, like chapter titles in more tenacious works, and frequently includes second-level or section titles inside the chapters too, and sometimes even third-level titles.

The depth of points in tables of contents depends upon the length of the work, with more tenacious works having less. Reports having 10 or more pages and being too lengthy to put into a memo or letter likewise bear tables of contents.

Documents of fewer than 10 pages don't call for tables of contents, but frequently have a curt list of contents at the start.

How To Do It

What is your unparalleled selling point? 1000s of would be product makers are competing for your customers. What makes you so exceptional? Here's how to compose attention grabbing chapter titles so you stick out from the crowd.

Discover as many search engines as you are able to and arrive at a list of the top searched terms for each one. Combine the lists, crossing out any duplicates. Designate classes to the top fifty most explored terms, like celebrities, research, finance, cash, love, romance, loved ones.

When the terms have classes, attempt utilizing them to produce your unparalleled "selling" point in any chapter titles you compose in that class. A unique "selling" point supplies the reason readers ought to choose your eBook from the thousands of other resources they could read. As an author, you're selling yourself and your ideas both to your publisher and to your readers.

Make it interesting.

Look through the content you have already published. Which ones bear the most traffic? Discover recurring terms in those ebooks and equate them to your list of popular search terms.

Talk to individuals you know. What subjects are they interested in this week, month, and year? Build a list of those issues.

Listen to the radio, study daily papers, surf the net. What issues are being talked about? Which ones return the most intrigue or controversy?

Utilizing the info you've gathered, produce your chapter titles that correspond to your subject. As a product producer, you're selling your services as a writer as well as your subject. You'll need to produce a unique selling proposal, something about your eBook title as well as chapter titles that grabs the reader and makes him or her take note. Utilize emotion laden, particular, descriptive words in your titles.

Utilize words and terms that make the reader ask questions. "How to Make celestial Au Gratin Potatoes" makes the reader wonder what is so celestial about them. Wonder alone will at least get them to click the link to your eBook.

A few style manuals advocate keeping tables of contents under 3 pages so they may be surveyed easily. As they lack the alphabetical format that makes indexes so accessible, anything longer may become hard to scan.

Automation for general word document.

Constructing a table of contents for an eBook is an automatic process with great word-processing software. Here's how to produce a table of contents and update it as you compose in Microsoft Word, as well as how to utilize the table of contents to scroll through your written document.

Make it a point that each embedded heading, if any, is in a discriminate paragraph by placing your cursor after the heading and pushing the "Enter" key.

Employ Word's built-in heading or outline-level formatting styles to the headings you wish to include in the table of contents. If utilizing your own custom heading styles, pass over this step.

Reveal paragraph marks after embedded headings by clicking on the "Show/Hide Paragraph Mark" toolbar button. Choose each paragraph mark, and then click "Font" on the "Format" menu. Click on the "Font" tab, select the "Hidden" check box and click on "OK." Hide the paragraph marks by clicking on the "Show/Hide Paragraph Mark" button once more. (If there are no embedded headings, skip over this step.)

Put your cursor at the location in the written document where you wish to construct your table of contents and click on your left mouse button.

Choose "Index and Tables" from the "Insert" menu, and then click on the "Table of Contents" tab.

Click on "Options," if utilizing a custom heading style, and determine a style you applied to document headings below "Available styles." Put down a number for the level of heading you wish that style to be represented under "TOC level," to the right of the style name. Duplicate for every style you wish to include and click on "OK."

Pick out a design listed below "Formats" or assign a custom layout. Pick out a tab leader (separator for the heading title and page number) from the "Tab Leader" drop-down list and the total of levels to reveal by clicking on the "Show Levels" arrows. Click "OK" to produce the table.

Page Navigation With a TOC

Scroll the written document to the table of contents.

Point to a page number in your TOC. Your cursor will switch to a pointing hand.

Click on the page number. The written document will scroll to that page.

Updating the TOC

Update the written document by appending, erasing or moving text.

Click anyplace inside the TOC. The table text will turn gray.

Push F9 to display the "Update Table of Contents" dialogue.

Choose "Update Page Numbers only" and click on "OK." The gray around the table text will go away, and the numbers will be updated.

Every format comes with its own default tab leader.

Utilizing the table of contents in that fashion will display the Web toolbar, as the table of contents page numbers are inner hyperlinks. To push aside the Web toolbar, click its close button if it's a floating toolbar, or right-click it and deselect it on the shortcut menu if it's docked.

Choosing the "Update Entire Table" selection in the "Update Table of Contents" box will reconstruct the default formatting of the table of contents format you picked out, eliminating any modifications you might have made.

Word 2007

Have you been tiresomely updating the TOC manually whenever you made an alteration to your eBook you were writing in Word 2007? Whether you have a written document already finished or are beginning a new one, a table of contents may easily and automatically be produced with MS Word 2007.

Headings and subheads

Determine which items you require named in the table of contents as well as their degree of importance. The degree of importance influences how the item will be formatted in the TOC. A main chapter head might be flush on the left margin. However a subhead might appear indented below the chapter heading to demonstrate that it belongs to that certain chapter.

Apply a heading 'style' to the points you wish listed in the table of contents. Styles are utilized to rapidly format any written document and likewise indicate which particulars will be included in the table of contents. For the function of producing a table of contents we wish to signal that a line of text is a heading so that it will come up in the table of contents. Open the styles menu from the Home tab on the toolbar or push ALT+CTRL+Shift+S on the keyboard. Highlight the text you wish listed and then click Heading 1 on the styles menu. The styles menu will stay open till you close it. Duplicate highlighting and clicking Heading 1 for the remainder of the text you wish included.

Travel to the page in the document where you wish the TOC located. From the References tab on the toolbar, click Table of Contents. Click one of the Automatic table choices that comes out and a table of contents will generate and mechanically come up on the page. If you wish to include subheads, duplicate step two but specify the subhead text as Heading 2.

Chapter 4:
Writing It Yourself versus Outsourcing

Synopsis

Are you a marketer or webmaster? If you are, you will be required to have material for your site. No matter what whether you distribute a product, build profit through affiliate programs, or offer certain services. You will need internet traffic in order to bring in a sale. Although anyone may choose to be an internet site owner, not just anybody can be a writer. And even if they are capable of writing, some individuals may not have the time or the desire to do so. It's not what you would call the activity of choice for large amount of people.

Among the most beneficial methods to generate traffic to your web site is with books, that is to say keyword books. Keyword books, when written correctly, are discovered by the search engines. This builds your internet traffic organically, meaning that a either a small amount of work or no work at all was needed on your part.

As well as adding keyword books to a web site, you are able to posit pieces of them to article or book directories as well. If you attach a link to every article or book, readers more than likely will be directed by that link to your website, creating even more traffic.

To Do It Yourself Or Not

Since you now understand how keyword books may aid in improving your web site traffic, perhaps offering a larger number of sales, you might be curious as to how you will be able to begin. The initial step is making a crucial choice. You will have to choose whether you wish to write your own books or have others perform the work.

Do It Yourself

Composing book material on your own is good, as it guarantees you get precisely what you need. Do you possess a mental image that's difficult to depict in words? If this is the case, even the greatest of writers might not be capable of providing you with the book that you desire. It might perhaps be better to compose it on your own.

Composing books on your own is costless, in terms of money. Saying that, your time might be worth revenue. Ask yourself, if not writing books what would I be doing? This points out an obvious profit to using outsourcing, spare time.

If you're constantly on your computer, searching for methods to make money, you might not wish to stop and compose your own books. Keep in mind, your time is worth money. If you discover yourself losing out on other good opportunities, because you're stuck composing your own book material, outsourcing might be the best option.

Outsourcing

When it comes to outsourcing for your writing, it's possible to discover excellent book writers that provide services for an affordable cost. This makes it possible for you to have someone write for you, without overspending on business expenses. This could leave you much more relaxed knowing that you will not be losing the majority of your profits by choosing to outsource.

The Pros of Outsourcing Your Writing Projects

1: Time consumption/ money savings. Internet site possessors will, in time, require an assortment of material. For e-commerce internet sites, the demands vary from press releases (to announce a fresh product launch), to merchandise reviews (to express to consumers what the merchandise is, its profits, etc), to commonly asked questions, and to internet pages. You might be skilled in composing a merchandise review, but you may have difficulty when it comes to composing a press release or a FAQ, therefore wasting time. Consequently, the best argument for outsourcing writing products is to limit your time and costs.

Many great writers will work for reasonable rates, If you do some research on an outsourcing sites, you'll be discover how many of them - and they're university graduates - will compose a 1,000 word piece for $5.00-$10.00. Even so, don't stretch your luck as when the economy gets well, you may be looking at a lot higher fees. When there's a dip in the economy, I feel that this is the most beneficial time to hire a ghostwriter!

2: Talent/expertise. Talented writers require only a couple of guidelines from you and they are able to churn out an article, write up an e-book that fits your desires to the highest degree. Since they are experienced, addressing the demands of a large amount of clients with individual needs ranks them high on the knowledge scale. For instance, if you said, I require a book with great SEO, an experienced writer would state, sure, just let me know which keywords to use and the keyword density you would like.

3: Overflow. You might possess in-house authors, but there are periods in the year that you're crunched for time. Independent ghostwriters are capable of absorbing the overflow of composition projects. As a matter of fact, the great thing about possessing your own authors and working with external authors is that you fulfill deadline dates and get the opportunity to determine which kinds of material may be outsourced and which may be composed in-house.

You as well receive different views and approaches to a subject, presenting you the perfect chance to accept composition that excites you and filter out those that are just average.

4: Flexibleness. A lot of authors who work independently possess several talents while other people concentrate on one niche. Authors who prefer to "spread their wings" also hold the power to provide other writing-related services such as proofreading and editing, submitting to book directories, putting up comments on blogs and forums, and spinning articles.

I've found numerous demands for spinning articles recently, and I've found that the same amount of authors are trying to get these jobs. If you're lucky and come across a well-rounded author who is capable of

completing tasks other than writing, and who's flexible, you acquire that added outsourcing bonus.

5: Mastery. Outsourcing your composition jobs when you've set a project management plan in place provides you total control over your suppliers. You get the chance to specify the kind of composition style you prefer, your submission deadlines, the amount of revisions you would like, and payment dates.

Sure, outsourcing to practical strangers may be a bit risky but the rewards outweigh the disfavors. Since authors establish a living from words, it goes without saying that clear and concise communications are crucial. The first consideration is how to articulate your task description. This should be to be the catch-all and shaping moment of your outsourcing.

Quality

It's crucial to restrict your business expenses, yet you likewise would like to pay for a certain degree of quality. This brings up another issue with outsourcing, quality. When you purchase outsourced articles from a ghostwriter, those articles become yours. They'll have your name attached. For that reason, make certain the work is of expert quality. To reduce the risk of receiving poor quality articles, request samples first.

Risks

The most dangerous risk would be that of plagiarized material. This is a great example of why you need to remember to check quality. Not only should you proofread an outsourced article searching for

mistakes, but also check its singularity. Utilize a program such as CopyScape. Never, under any conditions, pay an author for providing you with plagiarized work. Why? Because this is work that you can't use without potentially having some legal results.

Because there are a large amount of goods and bads to outsourcing your book composition, you might be uncertain as to which choice is most beneficial. You might want to experiment. See if you are able to discover quality book authors with sensible rates. Or, begin composing your own books. How long do you require to compose them? Are you turning a loss or consuming too much time?

Chapter 5:
How To Outsource

Synopsis

E-books are awesome for a number of matters. You are able to sell the e-book, give it away free of charge to build a list of likely buyers or build rapport with individuals, and you are able to utilize them all to market affiliate links and bring in additional cash.

However when you're running a successful net business, or if you're running the business in your free time only, you might not have time to compose your e-books.

Outsourcing e-book writing is among the simplest things to do now. Work for hire or freelance sites let you post a job and have it finished safely utilizing an escrow service.

You'll likewise be able to "question" or test authors prior to hiring them. You need to be sure that the author you employ will write grammatically and supply info that's valuable to your readers. They'll need to be able to remain on topic and follow instructions.

A Closer Look At The Process

The most beneficial place to discover an author is to go to work for hire or freelance sites. These sites let you post your want for e-book writing free of charge or a really small fee. Once you post your project you need to be certain to include the subject, the length of the e-book, and the aim of the e-book so that quality is controlled.

After you've based your project, freelancers will be able to bid on the project, and you are able to start picking somebody to compose your e-book. Bear in mind that the tinniest bid isn't always the best. You need to be certain that you have a writing sample, and preferably view an e-book composed by the individual. They ought to likewise have great feedback or references so that you understand they may meet deadlines.

A lot of individuals running a home or small business soon discover there are not adequate hours in the day to keep operations working smoothly. Better yet, business builds up and the need to find a freelancer gets crucial. Yet, it may be a bit unsettling or dreaded to trust a stranger with your company or buyers. With a little knowledge and planning you may pick out the correct independent contractor and outsource material to a freelancer confidently.

Finding a Freelancer

Construct a list of your business requirements and evaluate the price and advantage ratio of outsourcing work to a freelancer against doing the work yourself. It might be good to start with outsourcing everyday administrative tasks to let you use your experience and attention where it's most fruitful.

Think about the advantage of adding experience and natural endowment to your small business and project the affect on revenues. This will supply a rule of thumb for your outsourcing budget. If required, project milestones that you want to achieve to minimize unneeded expense.

Outsource material to a freelancer that's proven, even if it costs more, when there's little room for errors or neglected deadlines. Center on a freelancer's portfolio, references, credentials, and work history first of all. A few jobs might be worth outsourcing to somebody with less experience and humbler fees as long as they may evidence the ability to do the work thru samples.

Equate "Find a Freelancer" services in terms of prices, reputation, fields of expertise, and risk-assessment. Seek an escrow payment scheme that provides protection to both parties and keep away from paying a fee if there's no advantage in doing so. Get bids from 3 to 5 suppliers and equate qualifications and terms.

Choose a local freelancer if you're uncomfortable with outsourcing work to freelancers on the net or when it's cost productive to do so. Great sources to discover a freelancer include the telephone book, trade journals and occasionally the paper or net classified ads. Understand that the quality of advertisement doesn't always equate with great service.

Supply details of the work to be executed and any legal forms calling for signature, like non-disclosure agreements, if setting up to commit to a freelancer. Likewise talk about payment terms, guarantees and insurance matters before hiring a freelancer's services.

Make yourself approachable to steady communication to maximize success but prevent micro-managing or treating an independent contractor as an employee, both for pragmatic and tax purposes. For big projects set a virtual or in the flesh meeting to critique completed work or input on the procedure.

Elance

Elance supplies quick access to the world's top pool of ranked computer programming, promotion, originative and administrative contractors so you are able to get more work performed, quicker and more expeditiously than ever.

Employing on Elance is simple, simply post a job and get vying proposals from qualified contractors. As an alternative, you are able to submit your task only to contractors you choose. Employing on Elance is quick. In simply a minute or two you may produce your job posting and release it to 1000s of contractors.

You are able to likewise search our directory and call for specific contractors for your task. Elance helps you remain in sync with your contractors. With time tracking and position reporting tools, you have a fresh level of visibility to work-in-progress.

On hiring, every job is allotted a secure workroom where you are able to collaborate with your contractors and acquire maximum visibility to work in progress. Elance supplies a protected, hassle-free, and automated scheme to simply pay your contractors for results and hours processed.

They accept charge cards, PayPal and bank transfer. If you're a big business, they likewise provide payment terms. Sweep through the hiring procedure without lengthy and expensive talks: the Elance User Agreement specifies the work relationship between contractors and customers including, Intellectual Property, confidentiality, and conflicts.

Freelance.com

Freelance.com supplies both independent and consultancy-assisted manpower to businesses.

Freelance.com showcases the accomplishments of qualified contractors/freelancers to people in the areas of IT, marketing and communicating, journalism, translating, training as well as consultancy.

These people – or employers – utilize the services of freelance.com to help them assess, choose and recruit the correct contractor for each job. With freelance.com, both parties profit from the expertise of independent job directors, whose job it is to shortlist, affirm qualifications and support freelancers throughout the selection process.

They likewise support employers by checking over jobs, assessing likely candidates for the task, and ensuring additional communications and follow through between the freelancer and the employer.

This is the sole freelancing platform to provide the assistance of job directors, thus seeing to it that the bid and the job offer are fittingly

matched, as well as facilitating the achievement of the project itself. Freelance.com bills each party directly, meaning therefore that there's only one sole port of call for all administrative and fiscal jobs.

Chapter 6:
Dealing With People You Hire To Create Your Product

Synopsis

Among the greatest stresses for handlers of remote teams, is working with temps or outsourced resources. What are a few best practices for getting Outsourced workers, freelancers and temporary workers up to speed?

Tips To Manage

A great deal of the time we don't have a huge selection in who we work with, but we're yet responsible for assisting them in getting up to speed and working well with the remainder of the team and the organization. This is made even more perplexed by the fact that they may work for a 3rd party so mind share, execution expectations and allegiance have to be built rapidly and frequently from square one.

What are the matters that team managers have to take into account if working with outsourced help?

Worker's skill and tools/ability: are they competent in whatsoever skills you need for your project (designing, authoring, coding, search engine optimization, back link construction)?

Can they comprehend English language and communicate in an effective manner? Look to their record or portfolio, and references if conceivable. It is likewise all right if you have to train/teach the jobs you require accomplished (like running particular software or executing manual work). This will happen in nearly every outsource project. What's more crucial is the caliber of the worker; the cheapest choice isn't necessarily the most beneficial.

Worker's commitment: Does your project call for them to center solely on your job? A lot of outsource workers will attempt to work for numerous individuals at one time. It doesn't add up for you to pay them to work at projects that aren't yours. This is where it might make more sense to utilize results founded billing (per project) instead of by the hour billing.

Great help is difficult to find: you'll likely not discover your savior worker on the beginning attempt. You might have to try numerous individuals prior to landing one you like.

Don't get stung; always keep in contact through the early on stages of your relationship. Require voice chat on Skype to cover questions. If they begin falling out of contact or respond late and begin bringing in excuses, this is a sign of affairs to come and you ought to fire them.

But when you discover a worker you like, pay them promptly and keep them happy. You'll save much time and exacerbation by sticking with somebody you like, even if the rate of pay is somewhat higher than a cheaper worker.

What skills/tools are needed for communication?

Keep technologies simple. Google documents; produce to-do lists and portion out to your worker. Tell them to check over it each day or each week and move whatever jobs they've finished to an "accomplished" part of the document. The Google doc will forever be available online, and constantly up to date, easy but amazing.

Skype for oral communication; if they can speak the English language. Telephone them and determine how they're doing, communication by voice is far more efficient than by instant messaging and gives your relationship a personal touch.

Likewise, any screen casting software for showing instructional videos. You are able to go step by step on your own screen and record sound to explain how to finish jobs.

What tools do managers, particularly managers new to remote leadership, have to build up most?

Dedication to the outsourcing procedure. Many managers think outsourcing is a cost cutting process, and that the economic value lies in saving bucks on a project. They only look to outsource when they require something done. But if outsourcing is done correctly, you are able to automate so many of your businesses jobs and save much time also. Things like data entry, link construction, sort/filtrating/masterminding.

This means you are able to center more of your energy into more complex interests, like working out your business model, or how to acquire more buyers. This is a shift in the state of mind, as you don't have to spend as much time distressing about menial jobs, and center on larger strategies.

Chapter 7:

Developing A Long Term Working Relationship With The People You Outsource To

Synopsis

You might believe that if unemployment is high and companies are laying individuals off right and left, motivating your remaining employees to stick with you and work as though their hair is a blaze ought to be a breeze. However if employees who have already had to digest salary cuts fear that your business may fail or that more issues are likely, they'll be fast to jump to any occupation that appears more secure. If your workplace is ill functioning, tense, and joyless, they're likely to leave even quicker.

In great times or bad, your business will suffer if you don't keep the dedication of your most beneficial employees. Even as it takes a lot of small business owners 3 to 5 years to truly hit their pace, first-rate employees, even those who may do skilled work from their initial day, become more valuable each month they work for you. Long-run workers establish a valuable mental database of valuable info about your products or services, buyers, colleagues, and suppliers. If they march on, you lose everything they understand.

Your Workers

To amply appreciate how useful it is to preserve great employees for as long as possible-especially during tough times when you've no time to train replacements-think about your own kinships with local businesses. If you have been dealing with the same competent individual year after year, it's frustrative when that familiar face (or even familiar voice) is substituted by a less experienced one.

Hence how do you approach maintaining productive employees for you as long as conceivable, when your business is reducing and you might even have inflicted salary cuts? Begin with an easy fact: If your employees feel reasonably treated under the conditions and trust you have set a course to survive the economic downswing, they're far more likely to stand by you.

Treat-And Pay- Individuals Reasonably

"Fair-mindedness" is the best one-word prescription for keeping employees faithful to your business. Workers who trust your business may be trusted to treat them equitably are more than likely to be faithful; those who feel they're in untrustworthy hands are most sure to march on. This goes doubly when times are hard, unemployment is high, and your business is evidently scrambling. Allegiance frequently has less to do with the size of your employees' payroll check than it does with their notion that you'll do everything conceivable to protect their job, not just toss them overboard on a stormy day.

What is fair-mindedness in the workplace? Essentially, that your business utilizes objective criteria-not whimsy or pique-to give out rewards and penalties. Put a different way, it implies that your business builds and follows a set of work policies that are perceivable, consistent, and evenhanded. For instance, if you lay off a long-run, experienced employee but maintain your work-shy cousin, you risk convincing everybody in the company that in spite of your grandiosity about fairness, you can't be relied on. However if you adopt a merit-based system of rules of promotion and stick to it, even though it signifies your cousin is asked to go away, you go far toward assuring all employees that they'll be treated reasonably.

When it comes to wages, many employees utilize 3 factors to judge whether or not they're being reasonably treated.

How much like jobs in your region pay. Particularly for highly productive individuals who get just a couple of dollars per hour over minimal wage, it's crucial to pay somewhat more than your rivals do. Particularly when times are hard, you don't wish to lose the best of those clearly penny-conscious employees as they may earn an additional 20 cents an hour down the road. Regrettably, most small employers never get the picture, paying the industry criterion to the sales clerk who works doubly as fast as the average.

Once again, it's far better for employee retentivity, overall productiveness, and workplace happiness to reinforce your most productive employees.

How much other people with comparable skills are compensated in your company. Your employees will have no difficulty accepting significant pay disparities as long as in their eyes they reverberate true differences in skill, education, seniority, and task responsibilities. But dissatisfaction will rapidly surface if employees resolve that one person or group gets considerably better pay or fringe benefits for no

true business reason-or worse, for a sorry reason. This isn't the place to take on the details of perplexed pay equity issues, like differing rates of pay for different departments, individual vs. All-encompassing raises, and overtime for a few job classes and not others. But it's crucial to grasp simply how crucial it is even for employers with merely a handful of employees to produce logical, understandable, and defendable pay policies and modify them only if objective fresh elements call for it.

How much the honchos pay and fringe benefits are. Particularly when you're asking your employees to work super hard in an economically fraught surroundings, it's essential that you not offend them by exempting yourself from your non-indulgence program. And unless you're happily married to your bookkeeper, don't think you are able to pay yourself lavishly or payoff yourself with secret fringe benefits and keep it secret.

Don't Lose Your Purposefulness

Employees of successful small businesses are nearly always permeated with a strong purposefulness. It doesn't matter if you make or trade boots, Christian Bibles, or tubas -the key is to permeate your company with an allegiance to excellence, something that's particularly crucial to maintain when a business is scrambling financially.

There are a lot of time-tested techniques to help your employees trust in the value of their effort. But no sum of cheerleading will work unless they truly see that you execute a high-quality operation. For instance, if you claim your coffee shop has the freshest goods in town, but now that sales are depressed you at times slip a few day-old

muffins in with the batch, you'll start to estrange your own employees.

If you do run a high caliber operation, helping your employees produce and participate in a bigger vision will go far towards cementing their allegiance. No question it may be tougher to accomplish this when you're fighting for each dollar, but it's not inconceivable.

We're reminded of a vet who not merely ran the freshest, most efficient animal care process in town, but even when business eased off in an earlier recession, in reality carved out the hours essential to let employees participate in an assortment of free animal rescue and support actions. As a result, the veterinarian drew in a fantastic crew of employees, individuals who were so pleased to be part of a devoted business that many of them stayed put for years.

Communicate ahead of time and frequently

If individuals have lost work (or if employees expect to), a lot of your employees will be fearsome. Will they get the axe next? Will the business be traded? Announce bankruptcy? It's no secret that if left to fester, these sorts of worries may have a seriously damaging effect on your business. Productiveness drops when individuals are distracted and nervous, and your better employees might leave for what they comprehend to be greener pastures.

To forestall this, you have to honestly transmit how the business is doing, whether the news is great or sorry.

Value Your Employees

It's easy, really: Employees endeavor to do better when they recognize their hard work and originative contributions are noted. This is even more crucial when business is dismal and you're asking everybody for a little extra. In this circumstance, those employees whose great work isn't recognized are likely to conclude that there's no point in working so hard.

So whether you've 5, 105, or 1055 employees, build up an employee appreciation plan. To make certain your program will be received by your employees, it's best to produce it with their input. If you don't, you take a chance of acquiring a plan that will be brushed aside or begrudged. For instance, if your well-intentioned design to pay bonuses to salespeople who gain fresh business is looked upon as a cynical ploy to make your exploited employees stick in extra hours, you're unlikely to accomplish your aim.

When thanking individuals for good work, be as inclusive as conceivable. Don't acknowledge or honor simply the most visible individual or even the individual who's led a particular effort. Acknowledge everybody who added to the great work you're recognizing and observing.

Lastly, during hard economic times when everybody is forced to pinch pennies, it's better to keep your appreciation attempts simple, earnest, and cheap. A lot of rewards plans are configured (or at least appear that way) to influence or even control employees' future conduct, instead of to merely acknowledge their great work. Frequently a public thanks at a company meeting or thru email, or a lunch for everybody, is more welcome than a more elaborate system.

Lead, don't reign

Everybody affiliated with your enterprise will be more pleased and your business more generative if you're a frugal, tireless leader, not a favored dominator. U.S traditions are democratic, not dictatorial and masterful. At all levels of our society, leaders who work laboriously and are in touch with average individuals and command allegiance and respect.

If your employees consider you as a good human-and not simply the big honcho -they'll be far more willing to share their sentiments about how to better the business, something that may be essential to your survival in a severe downswing. To be sure a lot of their "bright ideas" won't be.

But after you place aside those that are self-seeking, have already been attempted and found deficient, or are simply plain absurd, you're likely to discover a couple of decent ones. And it's really possible that an engrossed employee who's authentically concerned about the future of your business will muster up a real gem, something so useful that it will make hearing dozens of average thoughts more than worthwhile.

Handle all ideas-even ones that are plainly nonstarters-with regard. Employees who see other peoples' suggestions minimized or discounted will be unlikely to make their own. You likewise have to develop a procedure to capture great ideas.

If carrying out fresh ideas, make sure you include key employees in the procedure, rather than handing down the law like the king. Fresh policies and operations accomplished with the input of the individuals who will have to cope with them daily are not only likely to be more successful-but they're far less prone to be countermined. Remember, employees who don't buy into fresh way of doing things may forever discover ways to counteract them.

No question, particularly when cash is tight and time short, it's simpler and for sure quicker to issue an order or enforce a decision than it is to hear, reason, and help construct consensus. However particularly when unpopular cuts are in the offing, it's crucial to launch and respect a consensus-building techniques. Or put a different way, a business that your employees deem as being all about you will not be as successful as will one your employees view as likewise being about them.

We're not advising that you make your business a perfect majority rule where all decisions are evenly shared. Leaving apart the fact that it's your business and you've the greatest financial interest in its success or failure, it merely takes too long for everybody in the kitchen to hash out how much sugar to place in the cookies.

Although a couple of cooperatively run businesses do well, we surmise their success has come in spite of the fact they promoted 100% democratic deciding to a new level, not because of it. Far better to run your endeavor with a secure purposeful center at the same time you ask for and respect employees' thoughts and treat them with regard.

Acknowledgement Is Cheap- Spread It Out

Hogging acknowledgment for the business's accomplishments is a major and common gaffe of small business owners. Even as professors are occasionally guilty of placing solely their names on research done mostly by their grad students, owners of little enterprises are far too prone to act as though they solely made the business a winner. Few matters are less satisfying and insulting to employees who have worked heavily and creatively to help construct the company.

Attempt to foster a culture in which leaders go out of the way to notice everybody's contributions. If this entails that your company meetings occasionally are everyone's accomplishments, so much the better. Individuals work more creatively if they recognize their efforts are noticed and appreciated- particularly when they're asked to work harder for lower pay and benefits. Here are simply a couple of ways to further this mental attitude:

- Acknowledge hard and originative work throughout the company-at company meetings, by companywide emails, and at parties.

- Share genial words from outsiders with everybody. If your business gets in the newspaper, or an employee does something newsworthy, e-mail the story to everybody and tack up the clipping on a message board individuals will see. If your customer service or sales individuals receive compliments, send them to everybody in the company.

- When a fringe benefit crops up, let the individuals whose work was implemental in making it occur reap the advantages. For

instance, when one company's site was proposed for a prestigious Webby Award, the hard-to-get tickets to the honors ceremony were provided first to the employees who worked on the site daily, not managers.

- If a buyer admires your work, mention everybody who assisted. If somebody worked long hours making your product-whether it's a paper, a set of drafts, or a custom cabinet-look awesome, notice that individual, preferably in front of the delighted buyer or client.

It's crucially significant to further a culture of "we," not "me." If, when the spotlight goes on, you are able to learn to step aside and nudge somebody else ahead, that's a great beginning. However to truly help individuals feel appreciated, you'll have to go beyond fancy terms and "employee of the month" type plans to show individuals you truly do value them.

Also paying decently, honoring superior work, and supplying great benefits, adopting an easy stock option or other employee ownership program can be the best way to virtually put your cash where your mouth is. That way your employees truly do know that your business is about them, not merely you.

Be Positive

When cash is short and you're chewing the insides of your cheeks with fret, it's simple to transfer your blue mood to your employees. If you do, your employees are successively likely to transfer it to your buyers, never a wise move when you urgently need them to buy more.

To prevent producing business-killing gloom, you has to understand how really encouraging workers to enjoy themselves may be a mighty motivator.

Here are a few ways to institute a cheerful work tone.

Food. Partaking in food is likely the commonest way to establish community. If you sometimes bring in a few treats (homemade is best), other people will, too. Make sure that when this occurs everybody in your business has a couple of minutes to savor the gift. If this means that it's your turn to spell the individual who answers the phone, do it with a grin.

Birthdays. Families observe one another's crucial milestones. Businesses bright enough to treat the individuals who work for them as part of a work family do, also. Maintain a calendar of employee anniversaries and remember to do a couple of small things.
Hats, shirts, and additional things. One company has a long custom of at times giving employees' jerseys, baseball caps, mugs, and additional little gifts. You may always tell that the general mood is great when you see individuals wearing them around the building or tweeting what they got.

Net businesses may not all be conducive to these ideas but I believe you get what I'm talking about.

Wrapping Up

Online business is a great way for small business and entrepreneurs to operate. Remember you have to do some research when it comes to creating products, outsourcing work and getting and maintaining happy and loyal employees and business partners as well as customers.

Hopefully this guide has put you well on your way to doing just that.

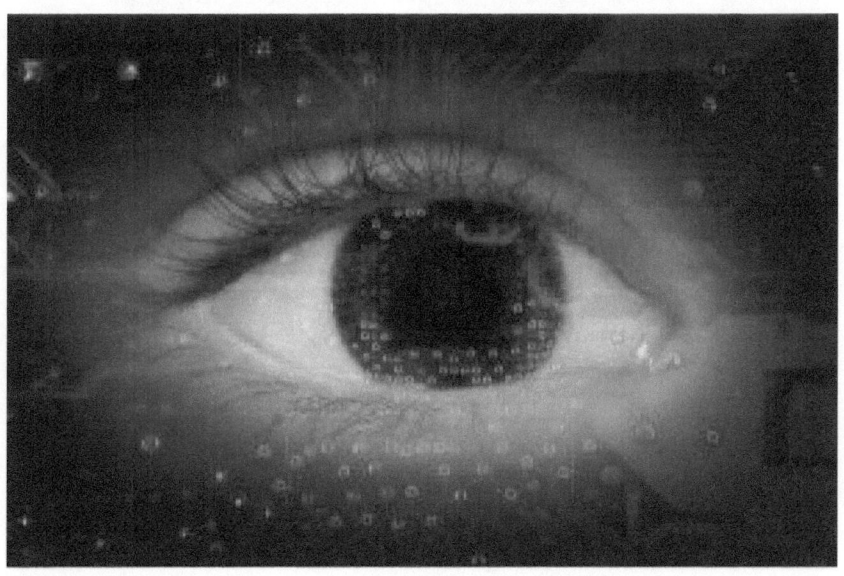

www.ingramcontent.com/pod-product-compliance
Lightning Source LLC
Chambersburg PA
CBHW020618220526
45463CB00006B/2618